SKOKIE PUBLIC

W9-DGP-319

FEB   2013

ARMY
NIGHT STALKERS

BY NICK GORDON

BELLWETHER MEDIA · MINNEAPOLIS, MN

EPIC BOOKS are no ordinary books. They burst with intense action, high-speed heroics, and shadows of the unknown. Are you ready for an Epic adventure?

This edition first published in 2013 by Bellwether Media, Inc.

No part of this publication may be reproduced in whole or in part without written permission of the publisher. For information regarding permission, write to Bellwether Media, Inc., Attention: Permissions Department, 5357 Penn Avenue South, Minneapolis, MN 55419.

Library of Congress Cataloging-in-Publication Data

Gordon, Nick.
Army Night Stalkers / by Nick Gordon.
  p. cm. – (Epic: U.S. Military)
Includes bibliographical references and index.
Summary: "Engaging images accompany information about the Army Night Stalkers. The combination of high-interest subject matter and light text is intended for students in grades 2 through 7"–Provided by publisher.
Audience: Grades 2-7.
ISBN 978-1-60014-874-3 (hbk. : alk. paper)
1. United States. Army. Special Operations Aviation Regiment (Airborne), 160th–Juvenile literature. 2. Night and all-weather operations (Military aeronautics)–United States–Juvenile literature. I. Title.
UA34.S64.G673 2013
356'.166–dc23   2012032062

Text copyright © 2013 by Bellwether Media, Inc. EPIC and associated logos are trademarks and/or registered trademarks of Bellwether Media, Inc. SCHOLASTIC, CHILDREN'S PRESS, and associated logos are trademarks and/or registered trademarks of Scholastic Inc.

Printed in the United States of America, North Mankato, MN.

The photographs in this book are reproduced through the courtesy of the United States Department of Defense. A special thanks to Ted Carlson/Fotodynamics for contributing the photo on p. 15.

TABLE OF CONTENTS

Army Night Stalkers 4

Night Stalker Helicopters
and Gear 8

Night Stalker Missions 16

Glossary 22

To Learn More 23

Index......................................24

ARMY NIGHT STALKERS

The Night Stalkers are the U.S. Army's **elite** helicopter force. They fly secret **missions** behind enemy lines.

NIGHT STALKER FACT

The Night Stalkers make up the 160th Special Operations Aviation Regiment (Airborne).

Founded:	**1981**
Headquarters:	**Fort Campbell, Kentucky**
	Hunter Army Airfield, Georgia
	Fort Lewis, Washington
Motto:	**"Night Stalkers Don't Quit"**
Size:	**About 1,800 personnel**
Major Engagements:	**Operation Urgent Fury,**
	Operation Just Cause, Gulf War,
	Operation Restore Hope,
	Afghanistan War, Iraq War,
	War on Terror

Night Stalkers are trained to perform their missions at night. They learn to fly fast and low to the ground. They don't want enemies to see them coming!

NIGHT STALKER HELICOPTERS AND GEAR

Night Stalkers need helicopters to perform missions. One is the MH-60 Black Hawk. It carries **special forces** and supplies into enemy territory.

MH-60 BLACK HAWK

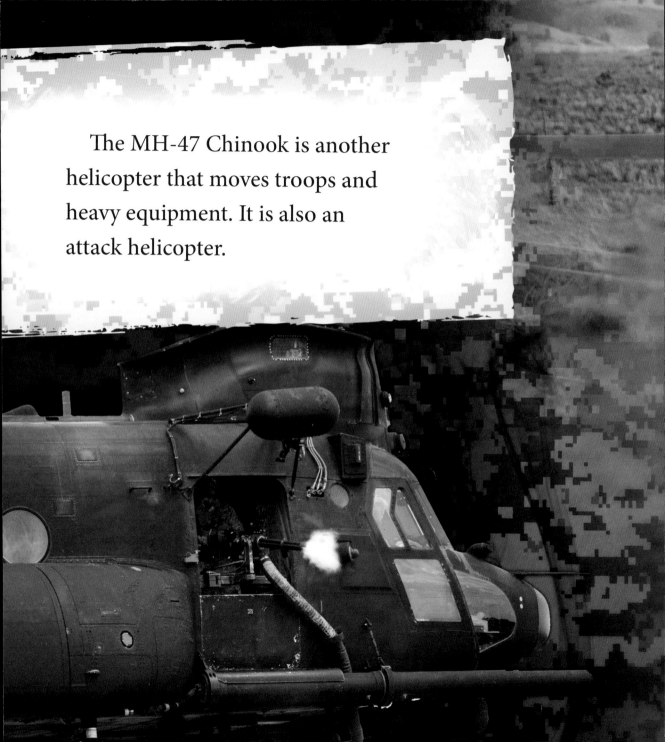

The MH-47 Chinook is another helicopter that moves troops and heavy equipment. It is also an attack helicopter.

MH-47 CHINOOK

LITTLE BIRD

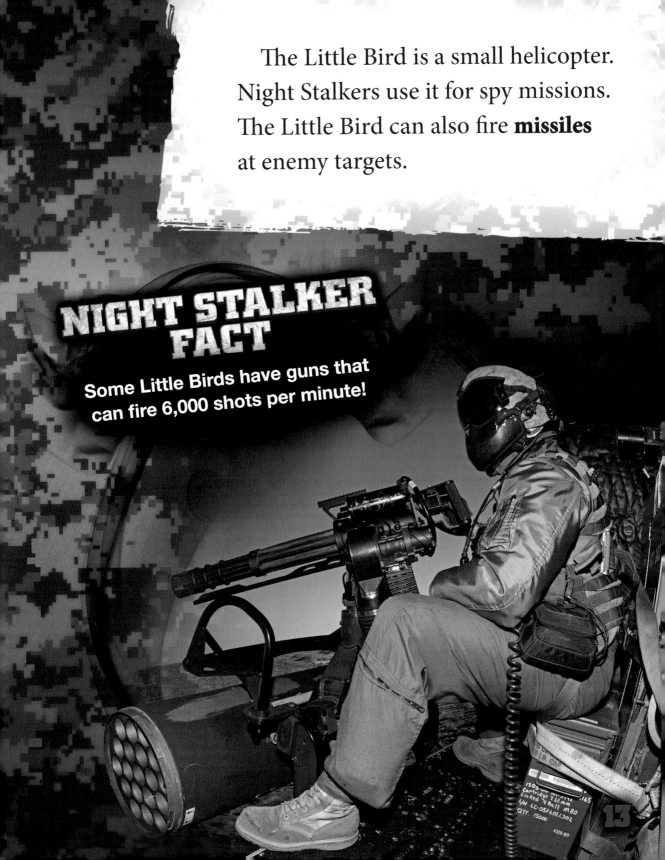

The Little Bird is a small helicopter. Night Stalkers use it for spy missions. The Little Bird can also fire **missiles** at enemy targets.

NIGHT STALKER FACT

Some Little Birds have guns that can fire 6,000 shots per minute!

13

NIGHT-VISION GOGGLES

NIGHT STALKER FACT

A Night Stalker completes about 100 hours of training with night-vision goggles.

Night Stalkers use special gear to complete missions. They wear **night-vision goggles** to see in the dark. The **Global Positioning System (GPS)** helps them find targets.

NIGHT STALKER MISSIONS

Night Stalkers perform dangerous support missions. They carry soldiers and supplies into combat zones. They are ready to help with **direct action**.

Night Stalkers also carry out **recon** missions. They gather information about enemy bases and troops.

Night Stalkers are prepared to fly anywhere at any time. They are up for any challenge. They never quit!

GLOSSARY

direct action—a mission that involves an attack on an enemy

elite—the most skilled

Global Positioning System (GPS)—a system that shows users exactly where they are on Earth; GPS also helps guide users to new locations.

missiles—explosives that are guided to targets

missions—military tasks

night-vision goggles—special glasses that allow the wearer to see in the dark

recon—a type of mission that involves gathering information about the enemy

special forces—troops trained to fight in small units with little support

TO LEARN MORE

At the Library

Alvarez, Carlos. *Army Night Stalkers*. Minneapolis, Minn.: Bellwether Media, 2010.

Hamilton, John. *United States Army*. Edina, Minn.: ABDO Pub., 2012.

Von Finn, Denny. *UH-60 Black Hawks*. Minneapolis, Minn.: Bellwether Media, 2013.

On the Web

Learning more about Army Night Stalkers is as easy as 1, 2, 3.

1. Go to www.factsurfer.com.

2. Enter "Army Night Stalkers" into the search box.

3. Click the "Surf" button and you will see a list of related Web sites.

With factsurfer.com, finding more information is just a click away.

INDEX

160th Special Operations
   Aviation Regiment
   (Airborne), 4
direct action, 16
engagements, 6
Global Positioning System
   (GPS), 15
guns, 13
headquarters, 6
Little Bird, 12, 13
MH-47 Chinook, 10, 11
MH-60 Black Hawk, 9
missiles, 13
missions, 4, 7, 9, 13, 15,
   16, 18
motto, 6
night-vision goggles, 14, 15
recon, 18
size, 6
special forces, 9

spying, 13
supplies, 9, 10, 16
training, 7, 14
United States Army, 4, 6